BLEMISH AND LURE

CHESHTA TATER

Copyright © Cheshta Tater
All Rights Reserved.

This book has been published with all efforts taken to make the material error-free after the consent of the author. However, the author and the publisher do not assume and hereby disclaim any liability to any party for any loss, damage, or disruption caused by errors or omissions, whether such errors or omissions result from negligence, accident, or any other cause.

While every effort has been made to avoid any mistake or omission, this publication is being sold on the condition and understanding that neither the author nor the publishers or printers would be liable in any manner to any person by reason of any mistake or omission in this publication or for any action taken or omitted to be taken or advice rendered or accepted on the basis of this work. For any defect in printing or binding the publishers will be liable only to replace the defective copy by another copy of this work then available.

Contents

Contents

Acknowledgements

You're not who you are without the people around you. They make you who you are. My sister, Chehak Tater, who writes beautiful poetry herself, has supported me greatly in making this happen; she tolerated me reading each poem to her (many of which have been removed because of how horrible they were). My parents have supported me greatly, not ever letting me doubt myself.

Mallika Dandekar, a great friend and writer herself, has given me constant feedback to improve my work. Tanya Goel, the friend everyone deserves, is the one to whom I owe the final push to make this happen.

Many other people have played big and small roles in my life, many of whom have becomes muses for the poetry I write. You know who you are.

Thank you to each one of you.

1. Band-aid

Air violins,
To dance in the rain
Of fragrant petals,
What is love?

To talk of her,
When not with her
Let her be the Sun
I revolve around,
She is love

To fix the intangible
With a band-aid,
Avoiding injury
By refusing to jump again,
Heartbreak is love
To smile your brightest

When they look at each other
Be a friend, wish well
No sign of discomfort,
Silence is love

Love could be endless

Or one without a beginning
Unconditional, obligatory
Fearful and yet brave,
In us, it stays.

The beginning

When all is bright

With bare minimum, you say

They are the one

2. Thirty

You read me
Chapter and verse
Hoping to swallow
In a single gulp
The years I breathed
Without your air

You try all your tricks,
The game of thirty questions
But I don't know the answers
I never looked at me
As a quest, as a book
To unfold

My poetry won't teach you
About my life
Or the secrets I guard;
Experiences that cannot be
Reduced to words
To be tainted by curse of a reader

Beneath my smile at you
Lies the pure desire
That one day you will answer better,

Know me better than I do
And words will never be enough
To sing our autumn romance.

3. Fairytale

You're a wonder, I don't know
How I got my hands upon you
A slight prank, a sleight of hands
Perhaps showered some fairy dust
And we were transported into a Wonderland.

Here there are no goodbyes to abhor
Troubles, they come, through it all, us stands
We're as perfect as when only one likes the crust
We agree that insurance is more romantic than a gesture grand.

They say it's honeymoon period, but they ain't got no clue
We met before we admit, perhaps years before now thousands
When souls, they meet, there's no question of lust
It's just a reality to live in Fairyland,
When the bubble, it bursts, I know you'll be there.

4. Sinking

We skip pebbles across the pond
Smiling through rippling reflections
Competing for the farthest distance
Unaware that it was us that won.

That was seventeen, now I scream
Until my eyes are teared up
Wrapped in your arms
Swaying on the rock chair of comfort.

You won't discuss bread and butter
Hate it when I say money talks
But for you, I'd give up the shiny rocks
Happily flaunt soda can tabs.

No matter how much we push away
Brush under the carpets
I'm tied to you, my rock
By the curve of the waist
Blissfully sinking into endless waves.

5. Week

The palette of my days
Surrender to shades
Of dreary rains
And storms that ignite
Passion denied

Each passing day
A heavy burden
On my feeble body
That lifts with ease kilos
And falls with a ring

What's the point
Of all these years,
Fake niceties, greens
When it's a curse
To wake each morning?

But I am living this week
Because the end lives
Up to you

I don't mean to impose
But you captivate my soul

BLEMISH AND LURE

With your vibrant prose
Colour my life
With your sunset hues

Six days of torture
I'd do it all again
For an hour with you.

Nothing is greater than love

But to have a platonic pull

Puts to shame

The great romance

6. Simplicity

There's no memory of you
From when we were two
We didn't grow up together
In the traditional sense

We didn't share secrets
On sleepover past midnight
I never cried upon your shoulder
You never told me what ached your heart

We didn't do it like in the movies
But we felt the warmth
On a breezy spring day
By the promenade

You are the face of comfort
A chosen dream to return to
Shop talk, rant and laughter

We kept it simple
They may call it superficial
They could say it's fake

All I know, it's not stereotypical

But I can count on you
On the worst of my days.

7. Happiness

My happiness, a stranger
Unaware one person could be a life-changer,
In one room but no conversation
Who could have told fights lay foundation?

I called you names
You wanted to hit me in the face
Sitting on the ground
Snarky remarks and acts unallowed.

You were out snooping,
Me inside snitching,
And yet we would find
A common fire, that burnt us alive.

With rackets in hand
Coffee secrets left unsaid
Who could have known
To make an End, is to make anew.

Quarters pass by,
Glee says goodbye
Until you walk in
New city, old enemies.

I keep a photograph of you
For when you change tides
For it is a rocky road
For you knew it all.

Life is all but predictable
You and I inseparable
Broken bones, kept promises
We are now accomplices.

We walked miles
Midnight strikes,
A slip of the mind
The guilt of the crime.

I wouldn't talk
Would hide, would stalk
But the notification still chimes
You haven't lost your smile.

An awkward jog
And to your shock
I say, I don't like your vibe
I took away your light.

They say communication is key
I thought it was begging on the knee,
But you saw past your greatest hurt

And now we joke over dessert.

You squint your eye
At a red flag you see,
I share 2AM stupid
Ask you to play Cupid.

And yet we are
At 6AM
Obviously, you're late
Obviously, with some gossip.

Now happiness is a daily friend
Oh boy, would I hate it if it ends
Life throws curves
But I know you can drive
Safely reaching home in the night.

8. No Talk

You wouldn't say a word
I can't stay without saying one,
A girl with milk skin
And a name I couldn't pronounce
Sits across, in papers knee-deep.

We would dive in
And eat our hearts out
I wish I could click every moment
And keep in my heart's pouch.

You broke my shell
And I gave you a new one,
We went places they refused
Running into beauty,
Running into memories.

What was I to be without you
Perhaps a little blue
Perhaps a wine drunk
Unswirled,
Perhaps a drunk swirled.

You could've been my inner circle

But you touched my inner soul
And those inside jokes
Those midnight whispers
I take to grave with my soul.

I'd listen to your silence
Play you a song
Maybe admit that I was wrong
But I refuse to plug out.

I'd fight to death
I don't care about answers
I want to tell you first
About moments that matter
No hesitation
No fear during admission.

You wouldn't say a word
But you held my hand
In the darkest affair
When Time slipped like sand,
Life was never then bland
And boy, was I glad.

Some may say it's the best

To be in love

But I bear witness

To never-ending anxiety

Of not being enough

To be the source of joy

For the one you pedestalise

9. Better Man

You say I make you a better man,
And yes, I do see the effort,
But darlin', this ain't no mission covert
And I surely not worth the passion.

You and I, we're from different worlds
There ought to have been no collision.
You and I, we are a fire tornado
No, we could never bring any good.

You're the Sun, I'm the Moon
I'm Yin to your Yang
Oh, opposites do attract,
But Poles they never touch,
Longing to feel the pulse rush.

No, I wouldn't lie, everyday is alive
Since the moment I heard your song
A love ballad to keep us warm.

But the Summer doesn't care
That lovers it may tear.

You serenade me, sway me off my feet

But I'd burn down your house and your dreams
I can't love, I don't know how.

You say I make you a better man,
Then, better man, you deserve more than that.

10. How

I create a metaphorical mess
Descriptions like similes
Draw parallelisms between
What used to be
And could be

I push you away
So, I can pull you back in
How I love, confuses you
You are one of simple pleasures
Words, touch, positivity in blood

How do I tell you
That I admire nothing more
Than your step within the room,
Your breath, your smile
Make my heart bloom

How do I tell you,
And live past the moment
Of grave vulnerability,
Without thinking of the worst,
Of a life without my darling.

11. Poem, for my Lover

The passion burns
In the blacks of your eyes
When you talk about
The love of your life,
Even though you have
Lost them a long time ago

Your poetry driven
By love, by heartbreak,
From disturbing screams
Within your soul,
The darkness you wouldn't confront
The blinding shine all can see

I wonder if my compositions
Could ever match your verse
Never have I had
My heart broken
Or even dizzied in love,

As you say,
Each line, each prose
Traps me in the imposter syndrome
I want to love like you

Even if it means
Encountering the worst
In my soul,

Even if it means to lose
The innocence I hold so close
I want to write a poem to a lover
And watch their eyes glimmer.

12. Muse

Your music puts my heart onto a blaze
Every note curing my anxious haze.
You laugh at your idiocies,
Never once thinking I find them endearing
Creating an impossible competition for every suitor in racing.

I never wanted a cheesy pick-up line
An illicit affair would've been just fine
But you told me, "You deserve a man of honour,
I'm ready here with grace, chastity and valour"
Now I sing, falling in love is an understatement.

Secrets and wine, blabbers and laughing
With you I wish I could have it all.

13. Goodbye

The bittersweet settles
When my soft-side battles
The resistance in my head
And the hole in my chest
The knot tied in my throat
From missing you like hell

The urge to reach,
I oppress
And tell myself
You'll call
And I won't answer
Not giving you that power

You are
Turning into a habit
And I fear
My need for you
Will know no end

Don't get me wrong,
My heart knows
You won't leave,
But what if I

Come off needy?

You like being needed
But I don't beg for love,
For attention
Would you not look at me
If I don't ask?
Would you not call or text
If I disappear for days?

It's easier to leave, to push away
Than to stay and show I care
So, this is my goodbye
To bad habits and needs
To the One who was never mine.

With insecurities afloat

What started must end

Only the one in love

Can be heartbroken

14. Diplomat

Would you file a report,
Would you frantically search
The lost and found
Like I did

Would you sleep in salted tears
The child of our acid friendship.

You didn't tell me you were in my town
I heard from another
But your mother
Still dials me to know your whereabouts

I have always hated to lie
But for you, I'd do it a billion times.

I was on your highlights
Now I remove you from the green circle
Hoping you'd notice,
You'd catch a fight

But you don't even give me a sigh
Pretend we are still on our high.
I wanted to call

BLEMISH AND LURE

But my ego was my fall
My faith was childish
Thinking you were flawless

You are the Diplomat
Never conceding, never blaming.

I swore not to be petty
But you get it right out of me
Please give me some closure
Or come back closer
Heartbreaks are not reserved for a lover.

15. Fifteen Years Ago

I can still hear the wolf bellow

Fifteen years ago when
I dressed in gray and white,
And my shoelaces tight
To a place I thought pure and full of light!

Never once I was reluctant to go
To the place Ma called my 'second home'
Until the wretched third of September
Of fifteen years ago.

From that day I would cry every morning
Stomach aches came unannounced
Just as the hand beneath my skirt, tickling,
But not a murmur from my mouth.

Months passed and Ma lost her temper
"I've had enough of your drama,
Now get ready for Vidyalaya!"
That day I spoke, for I was a sheep no more.

Ma asked me if there was a 'bad touch'
I told her of all places his hands had brushed.

Fifteen years ago something had happened
Then, I did not know
That my virginity would be questioned
That life ahead would give me a blow.

Nightmare on Elm Street became a reality
Only Fred was still alive (and happy)
And my hands were tied
By something called 'Society'.

Fifteen years ago
The tone for my life was set
When I didn't know what "rape"
But I knew how it felt.

In these fifteen years
I learnt how to cherish myself
To move ahead
To wear a shining armour.

How do I trust? They ask
It's difficult, but I believe
Not every corner is a wolf's
Some are of people like me.

16. Shooting Star

I was all but ashes
After a blaze of touch
Vapourising all my Sun,
I didn't want to live so much

You were a splash
And your cooling glance,
Baritone voice, reassuring
I'm allowed to have emotions

Step-by-step, back into the world
Sunflowers and no pool of hurt
But only if I could overcome
The breach of trust, skin and love

Your hopes and dreams
Were too much for me
Your positivity,
A rope around my neck

Despite the strangling
I wanted you, the care you gave
A new world you could show
A racetrack, a path away from the past

I'm not wishing that you'd die
Just wishing you were mine
Wishful thinking bringing
The monsters up from their hide

It was my fault,
The winds of my bygones
Hindered your flight
Spreading the fire of plight

I'd give you all my smiles
The happiness of a lifetime
If I could, I close my eyes
Upon the sight of a shooting star,
For a time before our fates aligned.

17. Sin

I paint you
My brightest skies,
Read you like
An instruction manual
No step to be missed

Be there
Before you call
To upset you
Would my life's
Greatest Sin

But you pass me
Like a cloud
Like I don't even exist
I could scream and shout
But you won't hear a thing

Maybe I'm the issue
Maybe I'm the one
To be blamed
To be sent to grey skies
To be burnt in fires
Alive

I know I'm not her
I don't want to be
See me for me
For the unmatched
Love I offer to please.

18. Ghostly Ring

Champagne glass
And a toast
Across the hall
I see you torn

A plan of escape
Bustling crowds hinder
Lingering around
But away from your Hero

Avoidance strategy
But I don't give easily
Confrontation,
Blame-game is on

"You left me, all alone"
A shared phrase
Truth, we dare not
Explore

You invited me here
To watch you exchange
Rings and vows
Yet you are in a spook

From the Past
I'm not a ghost
Just somebody
You used to know.

19. Numbers

I was four
When she stole
The toy phone I owned
The act didn't hurt
As much as her blatant lies,
I knew I had to cut ties

Then at twelve
I stood humiliated
At the feet of another
Who cheated me,
Tossed me aside
Like a crumpled piece of paper
In the bin no one cleared

At sixteen, I was told
I'd be left all alone
If, against the monsters,
I ever spoke,
If I didn't stick with my violators
I'd have no social status

At twenty-two
I'm sorry

If I can't let you in,
Say words of love,
Promise the trust,
Show the comfort.

BLEMISH AND LURE

If I can't let you in,
Say words of love,
Promise the trust,
Show the comfort.

20. Lean

Childhood pinky swears
Our fingers crossed
Fade away as masks we put on
Fight the world, you do you

In the hustle we come across
Sweet nothings, the One who forgives all
In the mundane struggle, with results none
We're bound to believe despite rationale

Don't make promises you can't keep
Make me lean on, and then shift
And fall from my weight
You knew you couldn't bear

To fall in love is one thing
To fall with grace another,

Some people make you better
Some prove you don't matter

To stick through hardship is one thing
To stick through cruelty another

Don't strip me off the dignity
Don't give them the impunity.

• 46 •

21. Memories

Airport goodbyes
Are the worst kind
Don't leave me,
Don't see my teary eyes

Apart and hollow
You can't fill the miles
With your vlogs and hi's
Even after a thousand dials

Post 3AM and an ugly cry,
I tell you what I decide
It is a sacrificial fire
Upon which we burn desire
And the fragrant flower
Of our lovesick hours

Sin is out my blood
But in my soul

Your parental dreams
I broke
There is no filial affection
No postpartum depression

No you and me,
All left is memories.

22. Cover

Our story is not a cliché
A backbencher, teacher's pet
A spectacled villain
A villain who won
A heroine who ended up alone

In friends, I trust
But never too much
For I learned early on,
To, "Will you take a bullet for me?"
The only true answer is no

I did what they said, kept myself from
Putting all my eggs in one basket
Little did I know
That all my baskets were tied
By a string of your name

Rumours work like magic
For I had the worst reputation
And you the best
Or perhaps it was because you were a guy
A straight-A student, dressed to impress

In my city, in my home
I eat lunches all alone
Cry until I run out of tears
Smile while facing my deepest fears
Violated, betrayed, lonely.

23. Caught

It was Valentine's
The best of times
When you don't want to be
Caught in fights.

Early mornings, gifts showering
Then us both together.
Love's in the air, smiles spreading
Caught in this moment forever.

Phone's pinging, texts a-coming
You're cooking my favourite.
Your familiar hands, unfaltering
Caught I'm in their lovesick touch.

A touch that has me in Heaven moaning
God gave His all to their creation.
Those arms hold me tight, protecting
Caught love in these palms forever.

My artist hands, creating
A world where our eyes are glistening.
I keep you by my side for an eternity
Caught between my fingers, a pen.

No, not today, it's not a pen
No, not today, is a day to fight
No, not today, is a day for her
No, not today, is a day to be caught red-handed.

So today, my hands red
So today, my heart faster
So today, my soul corrupted
So today, my hands red.

The Goddess of Love

I ask you, Venus

Is it easy to be a woman?

24. Moon

Am I the Moon?
Known for my beauty
Despite deep scars of my bravery,
Known for glow
But only from another's source.

Am I the Moon?
Everyday I am brand new,
Still picturized the same and blue
By lovers trapped in the pang and in the queue

Am I worthless without the power of the Sun?
Is it my blemish or my lure
That makes every Man to set his foot
On my distant and void soul,
A competition to his Muse.

Am I the Moon?
Only seen in the Dark,
Rovers digging up my existence,
Incomplete without the Stars,
Yet a part of every love ballad.

Am I the Moon?

25. Manipulate

Alluring and graceful,
A Muse with no comparison
But I'm no mere lovely,
Fair-skinned damsel
I'm the root of all distress and passion

I'm the glue
Holding you together
And even the pair of scissors
Cutting you, giving bruises
I tend to, later

The sensual parting of my lips
Perhaps an incoming kiss,
Or a bite so deadly
Either way, I'm all you know
Your world, my scheme

Don't be flattered, I make no effort
To entrap you in my luscious locks
I just hold the key you so desire
For reasons you're oblivious,
You come back to find an answer.

26. She

Where is she
Who illuminated
With fire rage,
Ambition for
Combustion

With incandescence
That knew no shame
Peripheries
Unknown to her
Rebellious, promiscuous

Passionate fights
No matter the cause
She couldn't be chained,
Be contained
Embrace her
Echoing laughter

Where is she
And her witty humour
Is it buried
Under the weight
Upon your shoulder

No sign of a smile
Unless to wave goodbye
To the apples of your eye
And to the one who dictates
Every move in the game

Once as wild as a boar
Now scared to be alone
You find domestic bliss
With a burning hole
In your heart,
Maybe in your home.

It kills me to see
You sacrifice
The dreams you
Left your love for,
Your brilliance shadowed
Just tell me, and I'll go
Where is she?

Where does it say

To love is to love another?

Why is some love shamed

Called names

Unnatural, narcissist, greed.

27. Lines

Most days
I'm a sunflower
Only good
When it's bright

Then there are moments
When each glow is a stab
Upon my existence

When I question
What good am I
In this world,
What's my purpose?

Helpless confusion
Surrounds me,
Reflections mocking,
What good is life?

So I tell myself,
The lines
On my hands
The fate
Not in mine.

28. Person

Young adulthood is not a rave
More like, being hit by a wave
Of sudden change
And responsibility

I was told I'd lose friends
Perhaps retain the best ones
So, it doesn't hurt as much
When she leaves

But then I see
I'm losing myself
Even in my own company
I feel alienated

This is not what I used to be
This is not the person I am
But both she and I know
The present is a better version

Then why,
Why does it feel like
A depressive episode
A lock with no code

A life, a path
But not the one I chose

I am broken poetry
No rhythm, no flow
Just existing because
I was created
For a purpose I don't know.

29. Inheritance

The whole family had been cursed since
She thought the King was her prince
Upto sixty-four she was lonely
Forever was in literature only,
But now love was in the cards

The smell of green was better than the perfume
Her husband sniffed off her neck in the ballroom
Her grandchildren laugh at the infidelity
Kids concerned with insensibility,
"Would she lose it all in Rummy?"

She would bite more than she could chew
Flirt with the whole crew
The newfound confidence
Didn't see the greys
Didn't care for the wrinkled face

It should have been a warning sign
That Monopoly got her blood riled
The greed was passed on
Casino wins or inheritance
Avarice is cureless.

30. Compare

You always think
That people more privileged
Than you, don't have it
In them to make it,
To make it past
The hardships you sail through

And don't people
From a lower class
Breeze past
You, with the reservations
With the pity stories
You didn't have the fortune for

The worst thing ever
Is to be stuck in the middle
The most oppressed we are,
You tell yourself
When you lack empathy
And the Courage to do duty

So, drown in your shallow sorrows
Be the victim of your thinking narrow.

www.ingramcontent.com/pod-product-compliance
Lightning Source LLC
Chambersburg PA
CBHW020753160726
47993CB00006B/2742